What the CROSS Means to Me

MAX LUCADO · KAY ARTHUR

CHARLES COLSON · FRANCINE RIVERS

JERRY JENKINS · HENRY BLACKABY

AND OTHERS

PHOTOGRAPHY BY ROB HOLT

HARVEST HOUSE PUBLISHERS

EUGENE, OREGON

Rob Holt's Dedication and Thanks

Dedicated to Verna, for the faith of her belief, to Dora, for the healing of her love, and to God, for His gift of the cross.

Special thanks are extended to Jonathan Ng. Jon's technical assistance is crucial and his belief in my mission is invaluable.

WHAT THE CROSS MEANS TO ME

Text copyright © 2002 by Harvest House Publishers · Eugene, Oregon 97402

Library of Congress Cataloging-in-Publication Data
What the Cross means to me / general editor and photographer, Rob E. Holt.
       p. cm.
    ISBN 0-7369-0615-0
     1. Holy Cross. I. Holt, Rob E., 1966-
BT465.W47 2002
232.96'3—dc21

2001038509

Design and Production by Left Coast Design, Portland, Oregon

About the Photography: All photography is copyrighted by Rob Holt and may not be reproduced without permission. All of the images in this book are of the same cross, the Valley Christian Schools cross located on the Diamond Heights Ridge in San Jose, California. These images are considered "straight photography," meaning they are not computer enhanced or manipulated, nor were techniques like double exposure, superimposing, or special filters used. What you see on the image is actually what is on the negative. The overriding technique employed is long exposure photography. The images in this collection range from a 1000th of a second (as in "The Glory") up to two minutes in exposure (as in "The Burning"). All these images were made with only two camera bodies (a Canon EOS Elan and an EOS 650) and three lenses (Canon 18-28, Sigma 28-70, and Canon 70-200). For more information about Rob Holt and his photography, please visit www.majiprints.com.

Unless otherwise indicated, verses are taken from the Holy Bible: New International Version ®. NIV ®. Copyright © 1973, 1978, 1984 by the International Bible Society. Used by permission of Zondervan Publishing House. Verses marked NASB are taken from the New American Standard Bible ®, © 1960, 1962, 1963, 1968, 1971, 1972, 1973, 1975, 1977, 1995 by The Lockman Foundation. Used by permission.

"The Gift of the Cross" is from Max Lucado, *He Chose the Nails* (Nashville, Tennessee: W Publishing Group, 2000). All rights reserved. Used by permission.

Printed in Hong Kong
     03 04 05 06 07 08 09 10 11 /NG/ 10 9 8 7 6 5 4 3

God forbid that I should glory, save in the cross of our Lord Jesus Christ.

Galatians 6:14 KJV

What the CROSS Means to Me

ROB HOLT

Photographer

The summer of 1996 was quickly approaching, and we had our whole life ahead of us. My wife, Verna, had just "retired" from her day job at the age of 24. She came home to work on continuing the success of our distribution business. We had everything we thought we needed: a house, new cars, money, and lots of friends. We were in the process of trying to extend our family when we learned how insignificant "everything" really is.

I had heard the clichés "Here one day, gone the next" and "The good die young," yet I never thought much about the truths of such statements—until a fateful spring day. That was the day I felt God's presence take Verna's hand from mine. Unknown to any of us, Verna had colon cancer. One day she was with us, healthy and happy, and then less than 24 hours later, she was in heaven.

I had also heard of scriptures like "His peace passes all understanding." And for that day and the following weeks, it did. I knew deep down that He needed her, although I wasn't sure for what. All I knew is that the power of His presence kept me calm in the midst of an incredible storm. It was painful but peaceful, perplexing yet purposeful.

From that beginning of my new life as a widower, those around me misjudged my reactions. Some mistook my calm for apathy. I couldn't help how I initially responded. I was the strong one that the family depended on. I had to be. I was the one who was constantly giving comfort and peace to those who needed it. Then, as time passed, an emotional vacuum developed as the reality caught up with my resolve. The friends I needed, the ones I gave my peace to, started to avoid me. I understood how it became quite awkward for them over time. They would see me, remember Verna, and get sad. So, I slowly started to drift away from everyone and everything. Eventually I lost all the things Verna and I had built together. The house, cars, friends, even the company, were no longer important. I let them all go, got a day job, and settled into a more isolated life. God's presence seemed farther and farther away. The depression seemed to be settling in for the long haul.

However, there was an ember of life still smoldering in my soul. I spent my hours after work, and almost any free time I could find, on a hillside. I explored hill after hill looking for new sunset spots with my dog. We became intimate with most of the best spots, as my only goal was to enjoy each sunset possible. I was mesmerized with the angelic scenes I found. Hours seemed like minutes as I couldn't soak in enough of a sunset. It seemed that it was the closest I could get to heaven, and it was the only place I wanted to be. Eventually, I brought my camera and started capturing the majestic skyscapes I found. It was the one thing keeping me from sliding into the quicksand of desperation and self-pity, even though that was the course I was still on. Alone.

The change that made all the difference happened when I found the cross.

My new friend Jim Ferguson took me to the Diamond Heights Ridge. Jimmy had seen the collection of photographic skyscapes I was compiling. He had come to respect me as I had turned away from the business world back to my first love:

photography. And so it was that Jimmy decided to take me hiking that spring afternoon, one year after Verna's death, to explore a new vista and a new vantage point in life.

I found many spots for enjoying sunsets that afternoon. But it wasn't until I reached the summit that I noticed it: a 12-foot-high, white wooden cross. What stopped me completely were the purple rays shooting up toward the cross. I composed a few shots, one of which became the beginning of a collection and a quest.

Back then, I did not see this new journey in the romantic terms I would later. I only knew that after looking at the pictures from the first night, I had to go back. Then, after seeing the images from the second, third, and fourth visits, an obsession developed. On an artistic level, I became addicted to the joy of capturing completely different images of the same cross. On a spiritual level, something was drawing me.

Words cannot adequately describe it except to say it was a very sweet Spirit of peace. I grew to love the experience of shooting the cross, soaking in a sunset, and communing with God. I had found my "quiet place," a secret place away from the cares, worries, and pain of this world. Before, when I was simply chasing skyscapes, I was constantly searching. I would always move from hill to hill, never settling on one location. But this spot on Diamond Heights became my new home. It was my place of introspection, recalibration, and reconnection.

While I did shoot some sunrises and midday shots, I would usually arrive about an hour or two before sunset. Some nights I would read the sky ahead of time and could tell it was about to "go off." Other nights I would be at home, look up, and see it "going off" and then charge up there. Sometimes, however, I just simply longed for God's Spirit and wanted to be there, regardless. Those were the most fulfilling nights of all, when I could get things off my chest. The most challenging nights, of course, were the nights I would chase the light, sprinting up the hill as fast as my legs would take me, racing to get there before the colors changed. On nights like these, I would get to the base of the cross, survey the sky and the landscape, and then quickly decide what my initial composition would be. Sometimes I would keep recomposing until I felt satisfied. Then, and only then, could I relax and realize that, yes, I was again at the foot of the

The Beginning

cross. I could begin to enjoy the view I so desperately wanted to capture and to communicate with the Spirit who brought me there.

And so it went, night after night, for more than two years. The cross became my sanctuary, my place of submission and consecration. The cross became a bridge for me. This is what the cross means to me. The cross was the bridge that lead me from despair to deliverance.

From hopelessness to hope, from apathy to faith, and from feeling truly lost to rediscovering His plan for my life, the cross spanned the separation between where my life was headed and, ultimately, my breakthrough. What originated as a place where I could focus on capturing the spirit of the cross became a place where the Spirit could focus on me.

The cross is my bridge from Death to Life.

The Gifts of the CROSS

MAX LUCADO

*E*very gift reveals God's love...but no gift reveals His love more than the gifts of the cross. They came, not wrapped in paper, but in passion. Not placed around a tree (or beside a birthday cake) but a cross. And not covered with ribbons, but sprinkled with blood.

The gifts of the cross.

Much has been said about the gift of the cross itself, but what of the other gifts? What of the nails, the crown of thorns?

The Branch

The garments taken by the soldiers? The garments given for the burial? Have you taken time to open these gifts?

He didn't have to give them, you know. The only act, the only *required* act for our salvation was the shedding of blood, yet He did much more. Search the scene of the cross, and what do you find?

A wine-soaked sponge.

A sign.

Two crosses beside Christ.

Divine gifts intended to stir that moment, that split second when your face will brighten, your eyes will widen, and God will hear you whisper, "You did this for me?"

> The diadem of pain
> which sliced Your gentle face,
> three spikes piercing flesh and wood
> to hold You in Your place.

> The need for blood I understand.
> Your sacrifice I embrace.
> But the bitter sponge, the cutting spear,
> the spit upon Your face?
> Did it have to be the cross?

> Did not a kinder death exist
> than six hours hanging between life and death,
> all spurred by a betrayer's kiss?

> "Oh, Father," you pose,
> heart-stilled at what could be,
> "I'm sorry to ask, but I long to know,
> did You do this for me?"

Dare we pray such a prayer? Dare we think such thoughts? Could it be that the hill of the cross is rich with God's gifts? Let's examine them, shall we? Let's unwrap these gifts of grace as if—or perhaps, indeed—for the first time. And as you touch them—as you feel the timber of the cross and trace the braid of the crown and finger the point of the spike—pause and listen. Perchance you will hear Him whisper:

"I did it just for you."

It Is FINISHED

KAY ARTHUR

It was a loud cry. *"Tetelestai!"* The earth shook. Rocks split open. The veil in the temple was rent—torn from top to bottom. Tombs came open.

"It is finished." The Lamb of God is slain. The debt of sin is paid in full for all mankind.

In the roll of the Book it was written. The fullness of time had at long last arrived. The Christ—Messiah—had come to do the will of God. The blood of bulls and goats sacrificed under the Old Covenant, the Law, could never take away sins. That's why the Father had prepared a body for the Savior of the world. The power of the Most High overshadowed the virgin Mary. The One conceived in her was the Son of God, born from above. And rightly so. Because we are flesh and blood, Jesus Himself likewise also partook of the same, so that through death He might render powerless him who had the power of death—that is, the devil.

Now it was finished. The cry from Calvary's tree *"Tetelestai"* —signaled a new way was open so we could come boldly to the Throne of Grace—to walk where once only the High Priest walked—right through the Holy Place into the Holy of Holies in the full assurance of faith. Hearts sprinkled clean from an evil conscience, bodies washed with pure water, could now enter His presence, for they were sanctified through the offering of the body of Jesus Christ once for all.

The Covenant

With one offering Jesus perfected for all time those who receive God's gift of salvation, making them holy and acceptable to God. Man's debt of sin was paid in full. Whether or not people choose to believe this, each person is now without excuse. God has provided each of us, men and women, an advocate, Jesus

*Satan hath found
has triumphed over him*

Christ the righteous, the propitiation, the satisfaction, for your sins and mine, for the sins of the whole world.

Tetelestai—"It is finished." The word rang forth a message of joy. Relief. Freedom. *Tetelestai,* in the perfect tense, means it is finished, complete: a past completed action with a present and ongoing result. In Jesus' day, this was the word written across every certificate of debt once it was paid in full. The certificate would then be displayed for public notice. Nailed to the door-post of the debtor's house so all could see and know that the man no longer lived under the constant weight of an unpaid debt that could make him another man's slave.

Oh Beloved, do you see it? Ours was a debt we never could pay, for how could the unrighteous, those born as slaves in sin, ever hope to attain a righteousness that would satisfy a holy God? Our merciful Creator understood our plight. Before He created Adam and Eve, He knew they would believe the devil's lie, yet He covenanted to do what was necessary to free us—the offspring of Adam—from Satan, who is the father of lies. When we were dead in our transgressions and the uncircumcision of our flesh, He made us alive together with Jesus and forgave us all our transgressions.

How?

In the apostle Paul's epistle to the Colossians, we read that God "canceled out the certificate of debt consisting of decrees against us, which was hostile to us, and He has taken it out of the way, having nailed it to the cross" (2:14 NASB). This, Beloved, is why Jesus cried, *"Tetelestai."*

...t out now, that Christ ...in his cross. Ah! Then, brethren, Calvary is a wonder in hell.

ROBERT M. McCHEYNE

But do you believe it? Are you resting the rest of faith, knowing that the forgiveness of sins is all by grace—lavish, extravagant grace? Grace that can never be earned or deserved? Grace simply and freely bestowed at no cost, without any payment on your part? Grace that can cover the depths of sin as water covers the ocean's floor, and still crests its shores?

Jesus did it all. Jesus paid it all. Your call is simply to repent—to change your thinking that there is something you can do, must do, should do, to make yourself acceptable to God. You can't. But Jesus alone could, and He did. It is finished—your debt of sin is paid for in full. Now believe and live accordingly. This is salvation...eternal salvation...the abundant life that He promised to all who would hear His voice and believe "it is finished."

FREEDOM

CHARLES W. COLSON

*T*he summer of 1973 was one of the darkest times of my life. I had loyally served Richard Nixon, President of the United States, occupying an office next to his for four years. Then came Watergate and personal calamity.

I watched the president I admired and respected losing ground, felt the prosecutor's noose tightening around my own neck, and saw everything I had worked for all of my life crumbling. Washington, in those days, was a particularly ugly town, the papers filled with charges and countercharges as well as political debate that was particularly acrimonious.

One summer evening I visited an old friend and client. Tom Phillips was president at the Raytheon Company. He had told me earlier in the spring that during the four years we had not seen one another—that is, while I was in the White House—he had an experience with Jesus Christ. I had no idea what he meant by that statement. But this August evening I decided to find out. I knew I desperately needed something in my life. I knew I desperately needed to be like Tom, who seemed at peace and happy and fulfilled.

That was the night that Tom Phillips told me about Jesus Christ and read to me from a wonderful little book by C.S. Lewis titled *Mere Christianity*. The chapter he read was on pride, the great sin, how a proud man is always

The saving powe.

depend

its saving powe

14

looking down on other people and other things and cannot see something above himself immeasurably superior—that is, God.

Tom wanted to pray with me that night, but I'd never prayed except in church and by rote. He prayed, I didn't. But after leaving his home, I found I couldn't back my automobile out of the driveway. This former Marine captain and White House hatchet man was crying too hard to get the keys into the ignition. I called out to God, asking Him to take me just as I was. Nothing has been the same in my life since then. Nothing can ever be the same again.

What I now know for a fact—and what I experienced that night—is the freedom that comes from knowing that Jesus Christ died on the cross for my sins and that I could be forgiven. If I did not know that to be a historic fact, I could not live with myself; I would suffocate in the stench of my own sins.

That night with Tom Phillips was 28 years ago, but in many ways is like yesterday. For hardly a day goes by that I do not think about the cross, the price God paid to save me, the price of my freedom.

I am so overwhelmed with gratitude that I can do nothing else but my duty in obedience to Christ. How else do you respond to someone who made such a sacrifice?

And I pray every day that I can live a life worthy of the sacrifice made for me on the cross.

f the cross does not

n faith being added to it;

is such that faith flows from it.

J. I. PACKER

The TRUTH and the LIFE

EMILIE BARNES

As a young girl, I didn't know of the cross or even care about the cross. Oh yes, I'd seen it as a necklace, as a symbol for the Christians' Easter, and on the tops of churches, but I never really gave it much thought. You see, I was raised in a Jewish home, and Passover was our day of celebration with our Seder Dinner. The cross was just two sticks put together.

However, when I was 16 years old, the cross came alive and had great significance in my life. It was then that I met "my Bob," who is now my husband of more than 47 years. It was this man who shared Jesus and the cross with me. Bob told me that he loved me but could not marry me since I was a non-Christian, a non-believer in this man called Jesus.

A certain verse stuck in my mind, when Jesus said, "I am the way and the truth and the life. No one comes to the Father except through me" (John 14:6). This little Jewish girl received the Messiah as her Lord and Savior. Then the cross had a significant impact on my life. Without Jesus' death on the cross and His resurrection on the third day, there would be no hope for the future. The cross was necessary for the resurrection—with no resurrection, it would all be folly.

Four years ago I was diagnosed with non-Hodgkin's lymphoma and the battle began. I went through more than 500

The Awakening

hours of chemotherapy and 21 days of radiation for a tumor in my stomach. My wonderful doctor gave me a 40 to 60 percent chance for living—and that was with divine intervention. We raised our hands and accepted the program. Little did we realize what was to happen during our journey. We ended up at the "Hutch" in Seattle, a world-renowned cancer research clinic, for five months of treatment and a bone-marrow transplant from a young, twenty-three-year-old Canadian gentleman. As the days were difficult and the future looked bleak, it was there that I realized I was going through nothing compared to what Jesus suffered on the cross for me. He suffered so much pain in order for us to have salvation.

Now when I see the cross, it reminds me of the suffering of Jesus—suffering so much greater than I will ever go through. These two "sticks" give me courage over and over again. Calvary is where He hung and died for me so I would have eternal life with my heavenly Father. This is a gift I will appreciate all my life here on earth. I look forward to someday being at home with God the Father, God the Son, and God the Holy Spirit. The cross means everything to me.

Nobody who has truly seen the cross of Christ can ever again speak of hopeless cases.

G. CAMPBELL MORGAN

The Heart of *GOD*

ERWIN W. LUTZER

oes God care about the world? I believe that this question can best be answered by taking a long look at the cross. Golgotha is God's farthest reach; there He came across to our side of the chasm to rescue us from ourselves. There darkness turned to light; hopelessness became the basis of our hope. The cross opens a window into the heart of God, and gives us the assurance that yes, He does care; and yes, He did "save us from our sins."

Never shall the cross be so precious to us as when death is near. For if we have embraced the Christ who hung there for us, we shall never really die. For He died, not merely that our sins would be taken away, but to prove that death does not have the last word for those whose faith is in the One who Himself conquered it. To sing, "I will cherish the old rugged cross" is not simply an exercise in sentimentality, but an expression of the Christian's deepest longings. The cross divides the human race in two: Without it, we will perish forever; with it, we are guaranteed life forever.

The Burning

The Old Rugged Cross

On a hill far away stood an old rugged cross,
   The emblem of suffering and shame;
     And I love that old cross where the dearest and best
For a world of lost sinners was slain.

So I'll cherish the old rugged cross,
Till my trophies at last I lay down;
I will cling to the old rugged cross,
And exchange it some day for a crown.

O that old rugged cross, so despised by the world,
Has a wondrous attraction for me;
For the dear Lamb of God left His glory above
To bear it to dark Calvary.

In the old rugged cross, stained with blood so divine,
A wondrous beauty I see,
For 'twas on that old cross Jesus suffered and died,
To pardon and sanctify me.

To the old rugged cross I will ever be true,
Its shame and reproach gladly bear;
Then He'll call me some day to my home far away,
Where His glory forever I'll share.

GEORGE BENNARD

He Gave Me His
LIFE

ANNIE CHAPMAN

W hen I was five years old, a preacher came to our rural West Virginia home. At the time we were an unchurched family, and the visitation from the local Methodist pastor was considered an honor. It was during that visit I heard for the first time that Jesus loved me. I didn't understand who *He* was or why *He* would regard me with affection. Yet, as a little child I recall being amazed by the fact that Jesus esteemed me a person worthy of His love. It was on that hot, sunny day that I decided if Jesus loved me, then I loved Him, too. Little did I know how important the precious seed of the gospel that was sown in my young heart would soon become.

It was later that same summer that my life would change forever. A farmhand who worked for my father tragically assaulted me, and the offense sent me on a downward emotional spiral. I became a very sad, wounded child who was left to deal with the harsh rawness of life. In those childhood years, I recall praying, "If there is a God, then kill me. Don't make me live with all this pain." The years seemed to crawl by for me.

When I was seventeen years old, I left that farm and ventured off to college. Though I tried to leave the troubling memories behind, they followed me and daily haunted my very soul. However, it was not long after entering the environment of a Christian school that my years of despair intersected with the cross. And it was at that "cross road" I learned not only that

Jesus loved me, but He loved me enough to die for me. Gloriously, we made the great exchange. Jesus took my desire to die and all the sadness that lived within me in and, in turn, He gave me His life.

The cross symbolizes the inevitable choice every human must make. "What will you do with Christ?" For some, that cross is a stumbling block that provokes anger. For others it is a nuisance they try to rationally dismiss. However, to those who have embraced its true meaning and chosen to walk its path, it leads to life eternal. There is no doubt in my mind, whatsoever, that had I not come to the cross, laid down my sorrows, and accepted the finished work of Christ, I would not be alive today. While the cross is a symbol of death for Christ our Savior, it means eternal life to me.

The Blessing

Back to the *C*ROSS

SHERWOOD E. WIRT

*A*s a young man I knew what I wanted in life, but what chance was there for me? I knew the answer: none whatever. I had heard about Jesus dying on the cross for our sins, but how could that possibly affect my personal goals or plans for attaining them? I failed to see.

Two questions, no answers, no achievements, no hope.

Then there came a time when God told me what to do with my life. He told me that because of the cross of Christ, I belonged to Him. So I believed, took Him at His Word, and life began to glow. But as many a sincere new believer has also learned, new trials come with time. I became faced with bitter disappointment until I wished I was dead.

One day I heard a preacher say I would have to deal with my problems. Of course he didn't know what they were, but he pointed me back to the cross of Jesus and told me what to do. He didn't urge me to carry the cross, he simply quoted Galatians 2:20 and added, "Get on it."

On my knees I did just that, while hands were laid on me. Thus once again I saw the Savior's blood shed for me. But a few days later I became aware that all my bitterness had vanished and I was filled with the Holy Spirit of God. Hallelujah! It sounds unreal, but ever since that day life for this nonagenarian has been love, joy, and peace.

The Power

The Message of the CROSS

ELIZABETH GEORGE

*I*t's time, girls! It's Good Friday. Today is the day we bake our cross-shaped cookies for our neighbors. First we'll mix the dough and roll it out. Then we'll cut out the cookies with our cross cookie cutter. And after the cookies are baked, we'll wrap up a plateful for each neighbor and decorate the packages. Then when Daddy gets home, we'll deliver them together to our neighbors for Easter!"

"And don't forget the cards, Mom," either Katherine or Courtney would remind me, "the special cross-shaped Easter cards about the cross that we always sign and take with the cookies!"

For years this was the scene in our kitchen each Eastertime as my two daughters and I sought ways for our family to share the Easter message—the good news of Jesus Christ's death, burial, and resurrection, the good news of Jesus' triumph over sin and death, and the good news of salvation and eternal life through Jesus Christ—with our oh-so-needy neighbors. Oh, our cookie-cutter collection included the shapes of a baby chick, a bunny rabbit, and even an Easter egg. But we chose the cross. Why?

Until my daughters "got it," they invariably asked me this same question: "Why the cross? Why not the chick or the bunny or the egg?"

Always, and in the simplest of terms, I tried to answer this question in a way that would teach my girls the meaning of the cross, the longtime symbol of Christianity and the death of Jesus Christ:

C - hrist, God-in-flesh, gave His life (Philippians 2:8) as a
R - ansom, a payment, for our sins (Matthew 20:28),
O - ffering up His life as a sinless sacrifice (Hebrews 10:14),
S - uffering unto death (Hebrews 12:2) to secure our
S - alvation from sin and death (Colossians 2:13-14).

Now, my friend, I have three questions for you. Have you embraced the Christ of the cross as your Savior? Are you teaching your children about the cross? And are you reaching out to others with the message of the cross?

The Declaration

More than a STORY

JERRY JENKINS

As a lifelong lover of words and a treasurer of stories, I have always been drawn to the cross of Christ. The rough, ugly vehicle of death for the Lover of my soul has become an object of beauty in the hands of lyricists through the centuries. I can never—without a lump in my throat—hear, sing, recite, or even run silently through my mind phrases the story of the cross have inspired:

"In the cross of Christ I glory, standing o'er the wrecks of time."

"I will weep no more for the pain that He bore; I will glory in the cross."

"Love crucified, arose..."

"Was it for crimes that I have done He died upon the tree?...Would He devote that sacred head for such a worm as I?"

As mere literature, the story of a sinless sacrifice dying for me would be a classic. The unspeakable knowledge that this is more than a story, that it is true, demands my very life.

The cross is the
center of the world's history.
The incarnation of Christ
and the crucifixion of
our Lord are the pivot
round which all the events
of the ages revolve.

ALEXANDER

MACLAREN

The gospel is good news of mercy to

The symbol of the religion

At the CROSS

Alas! and did my Savior bleed
And did my Sovereign die?
Would He devote that sacred head
For such a worm as I?

At the cross, at the cross where I first saw the light,
And the burden of my heart rolled away,
It was there by faith I received my sight,
And now I am happy all the day!

Was it for crimes that I have done
He groaned upon the tree?
Amazing pity! grace unknown!
And love beyond degree!

But drops of grief can ne'er repay
The debt of love I owe:
Here, Lord, I give my self away
'Tis all that I can do.

ISAAC WATTS

the undeserving.

of Jesus is the cross, not the scales.

JOHN R.W. STOTT

The Shame of the CROSS

BRUCE BICKEL
& STAN JANTZ

hile we appreciate the beauty of the artistic photographs in this book, we must always remind ourselves that the cross was not in any way attractive or exquisite. The death of Christ on the cross was not a pretty picture.

Death by crucifixion in the first century A.D. was a hideous sight. The torture, the brutality, and the agony made it the most offensive form of capital punishment. The Roman authorities used it only for the worst criminals. In the Jewish culture, it was considered a sign of being cursed by God. Friends and family of a person who had been crucified became the subject of ridicule and derision. They suffered the shame and scorn that was associated with the crucifixion.

The Jewish religious authorities that instigated Christ's arrest were intent on imposing the sentence of death by crucifixion. They thought that such a scandalous death would certainly put an end to His influence. And, in fact, some Jews could not accept Christ as the Messiah because the scandal of the crucifixion was a stumbling block to their belief (1 Corinthians 1:23). Despite the shame that was associated with it, the apostle Paul recognized that the cross was the best representation of what Christians have to celebrate (Galatians 6:14). We have nothing but the cross, and its shame and scandal are at the essence of our faith.

When we consider the cross, we want to remember that Christ had to lower Himself to the greatest degree to die a sacrificial death in our place. The real cruelty of His death was the weight of our sins that He carried. This could be no pristine and tranquil death; it had to be a horrible and excruciatingly painful death due to the depravity of our sins. We made Christ's death shameful and scandalous, yet He went through it for our sake.

The cross of Christ is beautiful and precious because it stands for the shame and scandal that Christ suffered for our salvation.

The Cleansing

I'll Never Be the SAME

BRUCE MARCHIANO

Actor Bruce Marchiano portrayed Jesus in the Visual Bible's production of Matthew. *What follows is an excerpt from the journal he kept while making that film.*

Journal: February 9

I hung on the cross yesterday. More when I have the time, but simply, I never began to understand what Jesus did for me until yesterday. And I still gained only a glimpse of the reality, the absolute subjection/submission to horror...for me. Every believer should wear a crown of thorns and hang on a cross for ten seconds—they would never be the same. And I can't help but feel that every non-believer would accept Christ on the spot if he did the same.

I have never felt so alone, so naked, so ugly, so emotionally bare—and I was just play-acting, dipping my toe into the experience of the cross. What He did for us! He chose it!

People were horrified by what they saw in my makeup and demeanor. I could see people all around me, disgusted.

Lying on that cross while people were huddling over me, being force-fed vinegar, seeing huge quantities of blood on my arm and on the ground. I looked at my arm and wept. Bruce read Scripture to me, and I wept. Waiting for lights to be hung, I wept. The Roman soldiers beat me, and I wept. Sitting alone in my loincloth, I wept. *"Eloí, Eloí, lama sabachthani,"* and I wept. And as the stories come in from crew and onlookers, I'm discovering many wept. What He did for us....Lives will never be the same. Mine will never be the same.

Hanging on the cross. It was awful beyond description...

*Every doctrine
that is not embedded
in the cross of Jesus
will lead astray.*

O S W A L D   C H A M B E R S

The Dream

INFINITY
at Its Best

JIM THOMAS

he central image of the Christian faith is the cross. A cross is the joining of a vertical beam and a horizontal beam, and it signifies the God of heaven intersecting humanity on earth in the person and actions of Jesus Christ. There is a sense in which the cross represents the Christian idea of infinity, because the cross can extend its four arms out forever. This, however, is infinity at its best, and it gives us a reason to look forward to every new minute we are given to live.

As long as the world stands, the cross will seem foolishness to natural man

J . C .   R Y L E

The Empty CROSS

TIM LAHAYE

Several years ago I wrote a book entitled *The Power of the Cross,* showing the transforming power of the Holy Spirit in the lives of those who bend their knees before the cross and by faith receive the finished work of Christ for their sins. In preparation for the writing I interviewed more than 200 people from all walks of life who were wearing a cross. Actually, I found it is the most popular piece of jewelry in our day. I asked each person two simple questions: 1) "Why do you wear that cross?" and 2) "What does it mean to you?"

The answers I received were amazing. No one took offense, and everyone had a reason for wearing it. Some cross wearers had no idea what it meant and said so. Some wore it as "just a piece of jewelry." One man said, "My grandmother gave it to me for Christmas, and since I am on my way to visit her, I thought I had better wear it." Many gave very meaningful responses—for example, the young schoolteacher who held her cross on a gold chain in her hand and said with tears, "It means everything to me—Jesus, who hung on that cross for my sins, died, and rose again the third day. He heard my cry for forgiveness and saved me. It is through Him that this cross represents that I have the assurance I will go to heaven someday."

I couldn't have said it better! For that is what the cross means to me—everything.

On our seventh wedding anniversary my wife Beverly gave me a black onyx ring with a gold cross on it. I have worn it now for over 40 years as a visible symbol that the most important event of my life was when I asked the resurrected Christ of that cross to forgive my sin and save me. Today I credit the thousands of blessings in my life to Him for not only saving me but also for guiding my life. And that is the important reason I prefer an empty cross to a crucifix. I never fault those who wear a crucifix, for they obviously are sincere and want to be reminded of the One who died for them. While that is admirable, if Christ had not risen from the dead, we would be, as Paul said, "yet in our sins." The empty cross reminds us not only of Jesus' crucifixion, but it also is a visual reminder that He rose triumphant over death and the tomb and is ready and available to guide us in the many decisions we must make in our daily lives.

Jesus lives! We do not worship a dead Savior, but one who is alive and at the right hand of God making intercession for us. One who not only saved us, but who is willing to guide us as we make the decisions of life.

Yes, the empty cross means everything to me.

We must do something about the cross, and one of two things only can we do— flee it or die upon it.

A. W. TOZER

When I Survey the Wondrous CROSS

When I survey the wondrous cross
On which the Prince of glory died,
My richest gain I count but loss,
And pour contempt on all my pride.

Forbid it, Lord, that I should boast,
Save in the death of Christ my God!
All the vain things that charm me most,
I sacrifice them to His blood.

See from His head, His hands, His feet,
Sorrow and love flow mingled down!
Did e'er such love and sorrow meet,
Or thorns compose so rich a crown?

His dying crimson, like a robe,
Spreads o'er His body on the tree;
Then I am dead to all the globe,
And all the globe is dead to me.

Were the whole realm of nature mine,
That were a present far too small:
Love so amazing, so divine,
Demands my soul, my life, my all.

ISAAC WATTS

The cross alone

is our theology.

MARTIN LUTHER

A REMINDER

STEVE CHAPMAN

No matter where I see the sight of an empty cross, the divine symbol stirs very real emotions in my heart of hearts. First, the thought that the original, blood-stained timbers once held the cruelly beaten body of the innocent Christ causes me to feel both humbled and hopeful. I'm humbled because the certificate of debt consisting of decrees against (me), which was hostile to (me), was canceled out and nailed to that cross (Colossians 2:14). I'm hopeful because I now have assurance, by faith, that eternal life through Christ is ever before me. Without that hope I would be helplessly miserable.

The distinct shape of a cross is also a reminder of other things important and precious to me:

- As if it is pointing in all directions—east, west, north, and south —and saying, "Come," the cross is a gathering place for millions of souls who are as needy of redemption as I am. Yet, the number of those who have come is far too few. To carry the message of the cross to the despairing is not just my duty, it is my joy.
- It reminds me to keep looking up. The One who once hung there will return again someday, still victorious!
- If the likeness of Christ is my target for living, the cross will assist me in setting my sights on Him.
- Like a key, the cross unlocks the treasure chest of the eternal truth regarding God's unfathomable love for me.
- Finally, the sword of the Spirit is the Word of God. That sword, ironically shaped like a cross, is God's final statement to the enemy of souls. "It is finished!" Blessed be the One who endured the sentence of the cross.

The Climb

The Majesty

The Measure of God's
LOVE

HENRY T. BLACKABY

Absolutely no words, or combination of words, can ever express for me what the CROSS means to me. Only Scripture can do this! The Scripture that has affected me the most is, "Christ crucified...the power of God and the wisdom of God" (1 Corinthians 1:23-24). Long before I did a research paper in seminary on the Atonement (the meaning of the CROSS and the death of Christ), I was overwhelmed by the personal search for the deepest and fullest meaning of the CROSS.

Then came the paper—and my life was forever deeply changed and shaped. The CROSS revealed so much to me: the measure of God's great love; the greatness of God's salvation; the seriousness of sin; the enormous and complete victory over the power of sin; and the fullness of life now available to me, and all people—because of the CROSS, and the RESURRECTION!

The meaning of the CROSS has affected my marriage and our family. His love has become the measure of my love. The CROSS has affected my entire ministry, and all of my relationships with people and my world. The CROSS revealed the measure of God's love, and therefore in all of my life has been the constant measure of my love to all others.

Season of the CROSS

BILLY SPRAGUE

For a long time, I have thought it one of the greatest ironies that we celebrate Christmas in winter and Easter in spring. The Christ child, the ultimate sign of life, arrived in the season of death. The cross, the most universal symbol of death, is planted in the season of life. And both of them seem absurd. God became a baby? And man killed God?

How can the infinite God fit inside a little baby? I witnessed the birth of my two children and held them as they cried out in glorious protest. My heart is not big enough to hold that miracle, just as my arms are not big enough to hold God. And how can man, in the highest act of arrogance, think he can kill the eternal God? Neither is possible. Unless God is willing. To be born. Then live and laugh, hunger, eat, thirst, drink, suffer, and die.

The cross of Chris bore; it is such a burden or sails to

I became a follower of Christ in the spring of my life, as a teenager. On an Easter Sunday I answered "Yes" to the questions Reverend Jones asked, then held my breath as he pushed me under the water and pulled me out. I didn't know much. I knew I wasn't going to live here forever. And I hoped in a life after this one. I believed and got soaking wet in that symbol of death and rebirth because of that hope. Now, as a more experienced sinner, I still believe but understand better that the cost of that hope was the cross. That first hope made me need Christ. The cross made me love Him. I am still a follower because of the cross, because of God's willingness, driven by a fierce love, to face what I have to face and to make amends for my wrongs with His rightness (that kind of irony is spelled g-r-a-c-e).

In the early summer of my life, I cowrote a song that would keep me connected to the cross all my life. It's called "Via Dolorosa," which means, the way of suffering or sorrow. It describes the scene that day when Jesus carried the cross through the streets of Jerusalem to Golgotha for his own execution. To my complete surprise, it became for many people a powerful portrayal of the willing sacrifice Christ made. I have

s the sweetest burden that I ever

as wings are to a bird,

a ship, to carry me

forward to my harbor.

SAMUEL RUTHERFORD

never stood on the Via Dolorosa, but friends tell me when they walked it they heard people humming my song. I still sing it often, and always on Good Friday, either alone to myself, or in an Easter service somewhere. (More irony: What happened on

Good Friday was good for me eternally, but so dark and terrible for Christ.)

I am now somewhere deep in the summer of my life. Fall is ahead. And winter. The cross always reminds me of my first Easter as a believer. It reminds me of the Lord's day of agony in Jerusalem. And it reminds me—and I hope it tells the world—that winter is not permanent. That it is not the season of death but of dormant life. And that spring, though not eternal in itself, is a revival of hope, a transition from death back to life.

The cross was created as an instrument of scorn by a world whose greatest fear is also its cruelest weapon. But in the hands of a greater power it became for me and millions not the ultimate symbol of death, or even life beyond death. It became the focal point of the great Love behind life itself. And it continues to be a marker, in my own life and in the history of the world, of God's willingness to die so that we, who would nail Him to the cross, no longer need to fear death. To face it, yes. But knowing death is not the last act on the last page of our stories. And with the freedom of that hope, life in all seasons becomes more glorious.

What may be irony to me is profound symmetry to a God whose ways are not like ours. We see death as permanent and life as temporary. But God knows that death is temporary and life is eternal. And so how perfect that at Christmas the greatest sign of life cries out in winter. And at Easter, the most universal reminder of mortality stands silent and leafless, in all seasons, still speaking resurrection.

Welcome, welcome, cross of Christ, if Christ be with it.

SAMUEL RUTHERFORD

THE
CROSS

The Millennium

Near the CROSS

Jesus, keep me near the cross,
There a precious fountain
Free to all, a healing stream
Flows from Calvary's mountain.

In the cross, in the cross,
Be my glory ever;
Till my raptured soul shall find
Rest beyond the river.

Near the cross! O Lamb of God,
Bring its scenes before me;
Help me walk from day to day,
With its shadows o'er me.

Near the cross I'll watch and wait
Hoping, trusting ever,
Till I reach the golden strand,
Just beyond the river.

FANNY CROSBY

The cross of Christ run whole of Scripture. MARTI

hrough the

UTHER

The Passover

One Got *Out!*

PHIL CALLAWAY

*W*hen my eldest son was only five, we were driving past a graveyard one sleepy Sunday afternoon. Noticing a newly excavated tomb with a pile of dirt beside it, my son pointed and said, "Look, Dad! One got out!"

I almost drove off the road laughing, much to the surprise of my son. Now, every time I pass a graveyard, every time I see a cross at the front of the church, I am reminded that "One got out!" Death could not keep our Savior in the ground. Jesus Christ, the one exception to all the rules, broke the chains of death, shattered our crippling fears, and promised us eternity with Him.

Most churches in which I have been privileged to minister have a cross. Some are carved into the pulpit, some hang on a wall, some are relegated to a foyer. But in Old Greenwich, Connecticut, there is a cross like no other I've seen. It is a sturdy 10-foot wooden cross crafted like a thousand others. But this one is different. This one is bolted into the concrete floor in the center of the sanctuary.

The preacher can't walk in front of the pulpit without stepping over it.

The congregation can't listen to him without seeing it.

A visitor can't enter without asking, "Why there? Why the cross in the very center?"

The answer is clear: For the Christian, the cross must be

at the very core of our lives. It is the central point of human history, and the central focus of all who embrace the Savior who hung there one awful day two thousand years ago. There was nothing good about that Friday. It left eleven men in agony. Perhaps they locked themselves away, asking questions none of them could answer.

Until that glorious Sunday when "One got out."

I sometimes wonder if they returned to Golgotha after Jesus ascended into heaven. Did they look at a gaping hole in the ground left by a vertical wooden beam?

I wonder if they smiled.

And if Peter laughed and said, "Hey, look! One got out!"

The Mercy

My Cup of
THANKFULNESS

LORI WICK

I tend to be a comparative shopper when it comes to thankfulness. I do this without a lot of thought. It comes naturally.

I might be sitting in the airport thinking how much my feet hurt, and then a man who has only one leg moves past me. Suddenly, I'm thankful that I have feet at all.

Or I might read in the news about a child who shot his mother, and just the night before I remember that one of my children gave me a hard time about doing the dishes. I rationalize that at least my child is not shooting people. See how much worse it could be? Doesn't that give me much to be thankful for?

Or maybe I'm thinking about my tongue, one of the things I struggle with since I don't always stay quiet when I should. But then I meet a new man at church, and he tells all about his years of drug and alcohol abuse and how he still struggles with temptation in those areas. As I listen I comfort—or rather delude—myself into thinking that my sin problems could be much worse.

Please don't misunderstand me. I'm not saying that I can't be thankful for the two feet God has given me, or for children who have chosen not to be violent, or even for the struggles God has chosen for me, knowing they are just what He has in mind. But I'm basing my thanks on some pretty shaky ground.

Enter the cross.

Enter the gift of eternal life because I believe in the Savior who died on that cross.

I never have to waste my time comparative shopping for thankfulness again. If I keep the cross at the forefront of my mind, I will constantly remember that I have something for which to be thankful.

I have eternal life.

My feet hurt today.

I have eternal life.

My children don't always obey me.

I have eternal life.

I forgot once again to control my tongue.

I have eternal life.

Having eternal life because of Christ's work on the cross doesn't mean that I ignore my children's wrong behavior or make excuses for my runaway tongue, but it does mean that there's a larger picture. The cross means I don't have to ache any longer. The cross means my joy can be complete. The cross means that confession and full fellowship is just a prayer away. The cross means that my cup of thankfulness can overflow 100 percent of the time, even amid upsetting news reports, weary feet, and a sinful tongue.

I can't honestly tell you that I am thankful all the time, but I can assure you that because of the cross, I have no excuse not to be.

God's Son, sinless and perfect Jesus Christ, took my sin and died for it. I know that I deserve a death far worse, but He paid my debt.

Even as I write this I'm smiling because of what the cross means to me. It means I have eternal life.

The cross of Christ is
the most revolutionary
thing ever to appear
among men.

A. W. TOZER

When I Survey These Wondrous CROSSES

STEVE BELL

We have several crosses lying around the house—a couple beside the desk at which I am now writing and one downstairs hanging in the dining room. Strange decorations they are, especially the one downstairs. It is a crucifix, which means the cross carries a figure of Christ on it. To display a tortured, dying man as decoration for one's dinner guests is kind of strange if you think about it. But, of course, it is not a decoration. My friend Norm made it for us. Norm is one of those deep-eyed carpenter types whose craft is prayer. I imagine he thought a lot about Christ as he carved it—and I imagine he thought a lot about us as well. Somehow, all of us, Norm, his community, and even Christ are represented as one in this piece of wood. That's how I look at it.

Hanging on the wall next to my desk is another cross. This is a smaller one, a gift from my wife. It is a plain square wooden cross with a figure of Christ on it as well. This Christ is not emaciated, naked, and dying as is the other one. This Christ is fully robed and upright—arms flung open, outstretched in celebration, in welcome, and in blessing. This Christ is not fastened but floating—held not by nails and ropes but by His own will—the will of God. He is *Christus Victor!*, glorified with the Father and the Spirit now and unto ages of ages. This one arrests me and draws a tearful, adoring "Holy! Holy! Holy!" from the deepest part of my being. This one makes me forget about myself.

"If God were good,"
says the world, "the sin of the
to which the preacher answers
"See His breaking heart."

GEORGE A

Lying on the shelf beneath *Christus Victor* is a cross my son Jesse gave me last summer. He fashioned it some 25 feet above the earth, while perched in the branches of an old oak that stands alone against a galleon of poplars. This cross is perfectly proportioned, made of slender, trimmed branches that have been notched and fastened with wire. I don't know what all was going on for Jesse as he made it, probably more than he even knows, but I am deeply touched that he thought I should have it.

Then there is, of course, the "real" cross of Christ; the one that exists in time but transcends any such means of measuring—the one in whose light all the others become mere shadows. But shadows are never only "mere." For some of us who may be too tired, wounded, or afraid to look up, shadows may be the only indicators we have of the real. Shadows always invite us to look up, if at all possible, to discern their cause. In this case, the cause is not the cross itself, but that ineffable, pure white light which makes every real thing visible, and all other shadows possible. Glory to You, O Lord!

arth would break His heart";

pointing to the cross,

Let the Hammers **RING!**

ED HINDSON

Crucifixion was a dirty business, and the Romans were experts at it. They did it all the time. It was their way of keeping the general public in submission. Still, it wasn't for everybody; they reserved this most cruel punishment only for slaves and foreigners. Roman citizens were exempt.

Dying on a cross was the worst thing that could happen to a Jew because such a punishment was associated with the curse of God (Deuteronomy 21:22-23). It was the ultimate humiliation. You were stripped of your clothes, battered by soldiers, nailed to the cross bars, and hung naked, suspended between heaven and earth. It was a spectacle of blood, sweat, and tears.

The steady crack of the hammers could be heard above the screams of the victims and the cries of their relatives. Each blow increased the pain. Each strike of the hammers told the condemned that there was no hope of release.

But as the hammers rang out against the rocky cliff, one steady voice could be heard above the clamor and pain: "Father, forgive them; for they know not what they do" (Luke 23:34 KJV).

Even in this awful moment, Jesus would rise above it all. Here at the Place of the Skull we see no squirming, squealing victim—no angry, cursing man. We see the Savior in all His greatness, goodness, and compassion. We see Him forgiving His unsuspecting executioners.

Let the hammers ring! For in their ugly sound we hear the grace of God shouting above it all. From the very throne of God, through the canyon of eternity, comes the one word of hope for all mankind—*grace!*

The Redemption

As they were looking on

gaze on His wounds as He hang

blood as He dies.   We see the

the redeemer, touch the scars of His

He bows His head, as if to kiss you.

His heart is made bare open, as it

you.   His arms are extended that

you.   His whole body is displayed for

Ponder how great these things ar

be rightly weighed in your mind: as H

the cross in every part of His bod

may now be fixed in every par

AUGUSTINE OF HIPPO

so we too

We see His

price offered by

resurrection.

...ere, in love to

He may embrace

your redemption.

Let all this

as once fixed to

for you, so He

of your soul.

The Breakthrough

Blood-bought *G*RACE

T. M. MOORE

*A*round the wretched blood-bathed tree a crowd
of angry mockers taunts the battered King
of Love. Their raw reproaches form a loud

cacophony of scorn, and bite and sting
in voices strangely like my own. A troop
of soldiers gambles for the only thing

He owns, and I am in that grisly group.
He thirsts. One races in a gait like mine
to thrust upon His pained, parched lips a soup

comprised of sour herbs and bitter wine.
The darkness falls, like that which fills my soul.
As shame-faced day gives way to a divine

outpouring of eternal wrath, the whole
creation groans. Meanwhile, behind the veil
that shades the spirit realm, the demons roll

and tumble, stumbling in defeat. They wail
and shriek, but all to no avail, their doom
as sure as my forgiveness. As the trail

of blood flows to the earth, a garden tomb
awaits its unintentioned Guest, and I
will be among the ones who seal that room

*Nothing in my
hand I bring,
Simply to Thy
cross I cling.*

AUGUSTUS M.
TOPLADY

as though that were the end of that. Now by
the Holy Place divine archangels stand
to rend the separating curtain high

to low, and open up for every man
and woman—even such as I—the place
of glory and the blessed promised land,

where I behold the risen Savior's face
and bow and bask within His blood-bought grace.

The Joy to Come

BECKY FREEMAN

When I think of the cross, I think of the hope-filled words about Jesus from the writer of Hebrews: "Let us fix our eyes on Jesus, the author and perfecter of our faith, who for the joy set before him endured the cross, scorning its shame, and sat down at the right hand of the throne of God. Consider him who endured such opposition from sinful men, so that you will not grow weary and lose heart" (Hebrews 12:2-3).

These verses remind me of a woman in labor who endures the agony of birth pangs, the water breaking, and the blood flowing by focusing on the joy to come—the precious face of her soon-to-be-born baby.

Christ endured the agony of the cross as He labored for the joy to come—the faces of His children, newly born into the Father's arms.

"Suffering," wrote W.E. Vine, "increases our capacity for joy." Isn't that profoundly true? Almost every deep joy is preceded by some sort of suffering and often a time of sheer, dogged endurance.

When I wonder how my Savior endured the tauntings, the thorns, the torture of the cross, I remember that His spiritual eyes stayed glued on the joy to come, on faces newly born, free from sin, made innocent by the water and blood that flowed from His side. And I am humbled with awe and gratitude to be one of the faces He died for. My joy-to-come held Him fast to the cross, when at any moment He could have torn Himself away from the agonizing scene and flown to heaven's safety.

When I grow world weary, when moments come to me, as they do to all of us, where my grief is so heavy that the very best I can do is simply endure the hours, I find comfort by turning my spiritual eyes to my Beloved Focal Point: Jesus Himself—and the joy to come.

The Way

A Rare
SACRIFICE

RAY PRITCHARD

Very rarely will anyone die for a righteous man, though
for a good man someone might possibly dare to die.
Romans 5:7

How many people are you willing to die for? If the chips were down, the moment came, and in a split second you had to make a decision, how many people would you be willing to lay down your life for—with no hesitation or reservation? For most of us, the list would be small indeed. Your parents, your children, your husband or wife, and perhaps one or two very close friends. But that's about it. As I thought about it, my list is very small. In the first place, you never know until the moment comes, and you pray never to be put in that agonizing position. But what if you were?

At the cross God wrapped and let it be nailed

We've all read those heroic stories where someone gives his life to save a stranger. This week I read a story about a mining disaster. Two men were trapped in a mine. They had two oxygen masks but one had been broken in the collapse of the walls. One man said to the other, "You take it. You've got a wife and children. I don't have anybody. I can go. You've got to stay." The one man voluntarily died so the other might live.

When we hear a story like that, we feel as if we're standing on holy ground. And indeed we are, for such sacrifice is rare indeed.

As great as that kind of love is, which is described in Romans 5:7, God's love is much greater. God went far beyond what we or any person might do—sacrificing our life for another person. We would never think of doing what He did. The wonder of the gospel is not that Christ should die for us— though that would be wonderful enough. The wonder is that Christ died for us while we were still sinners, still ungodly, still powerless, and still enemies of God! He didn't die for His friends. He died for His enemies. He died for those who crucified Him. He died for those who hated Him. He died for those who rejected Him. He died for those who cheered as the nails were driven in His hands. We would never do anything like that! We might die for our friends, but never for our enemies. But that's what Jesus did for us.

His heart in flesh and blood

'o the cross for our redemption.

E. STANLEY JONES

One day when I felt lonely I asked, "Lord, how much do You love me?"

"This much," He replied. Then He stretched out His arms, bowed His head, and died.

The Revelation

A FORGIVEN
Person

BOB GEORGE

*W*hen Jesus declared from the cross, "It is finished," I want to think that He meant what He said. What impact do those words have on your life? What kind of a person are you as a result of those words? Are you a person *capable* of receiving forgiveness, or are you a *forgiven* person?

I hope you answered that you're a forgiven person. The divine debt for our sins is paid for—finished! So what does faith say to this fact? It says with gratefulness of heart, "Oh Lord, thank You that I am forever forgiven in Your sight because of Jesus!"

Paul tells us, "In him we have redemption through his blood, the forgiveness of sins, in accordance with the riches of God's grace" (Ephesians 1:7). According to this verse, if you are in Christ, you have forgiveness of sins. It is your present possession and because of this you are a forgiven person. Rest in it.

When I first realized this tremendous truth, I can't describe the sense of rest that came in to my heart. The completeness of my salvation overwhelmed me. It still does. Though it's been many years since I came to understand the work of the cross, I still find myself asking, "Lord, who am I that You should be mindful of me?"

The cross is no longer a doctrine in my life—it's life itself. In God's eyes my forgiveness and redemption is an absolute, not a relative fact.

And so is yours. And God wants us to rest in what is finished by Him.

Christ Jesus has done it all. He took away our sins eternally so that He could provide to us a life that is eternal—His life. And because of His sacrifice, we can know that we have eternal life.

Yet, we forget and fall back into self-effort. Our habit of asking for more forgiveness, more redemption, more righteousness, more sanctification has to be replaced with a habit of trusting Him. He has done everything for us. Living by faith in this truth is what pleases Him.

If you've never stopped to ponder how great your salvation is, I want you to take a few moments and thank God for *your* complete, finished, and perfect salvation. You are loved and accepted unconditionally by God. Because of His completed work on the cross, you are a forgiven person and can enjoy the abundant life you have in Him.

The Separation

The Mystery of the Cross

JOHN H. ARMSTRONG

Consistently the New Testament speaks of the cross of Christ as "an offense." More literally, the word means "scandal." It would appear that the entirety of the Christian life and, for that matter, all sound theology should be summarized as "the scandal of the cross." This is surely why Paul considered all knowledge to be nothing in the light of the mystery of the cross.

But why? The cross was a Roman torture stake, a place of cruel and horrific death. Yet it became the divinely given word which summed up the entire faith and life of the follower of Jesus Christ. Ponder the crux of this amazing revelation. This cross, a source of embarrassment and provocation for all who do not believe the good news of Christ's sacrifice for the world, becomes for those who are called by God "the power of God." To the Jews, the cross was a mark of disgrace. Here a man accursed by God, indeed totally abandoned by God, died an ignominious death. To the Romans, the cross was a symbol of total defeat, a contemptuous display of loathing and complete loss. To the Greek, the cross was a sign of disgust, standing against the perfectibility of the human person. But the Christian sees in the same cross, in a divine mystery, the wisdom, grace, strength, and power of God Himself. This is why the Christian delights, or "boasts," in the cross of Jesus *alone*.

Here is the mystery of true godliness. What the world ultimately counts as nothing but weakness and foolishness, the Christian sees by divine unveiling as hope—hope in the face of life's deepest challenges and death's sullen streams. Here, at the cross, human pride is finally conquered by divine grace. Here all human effort to gain redemption by our own effort comes to an abrupt end. Here the redeemed die to themselves daily and to all their petty dreams of temporal success. Here the believer looks, and looks, and keeps on looking, for an entire lifetime. With the hymn writer, the one who looks with real trust in the Son of God will confess:

> Upon the cross of Jesus, mine eye at times can see;
> The very dying form of One, who suffered there for me,
> And from my stricken heart with tears, two wonders I
>   confess;
> The wonders of redeeming love and my own worthlessness.

Another hymn writer summarizes our only adequate response to the cross of Jesus Christ:

> But drops of grief can ne'er repay
> The debt of love I owe;
> Here, Lord, I give myself away,
> 'Tis all that I can do.

In the cross is salvation, in the cross is life, in the cross is protection against our enemies, in the cross is infusion of heavenly sweetness, in the cross is strength of mind, in the cross joy of spirit, in the cross the height of virtue, in the cross the perfection of sanctity.

There is no salvation of the soul, nor hope of everlasting life, but in the cross.

Take up therefore thy cross and follow Jesus, and thou shalt go into life everlasting. He went before, bearing His cross, and died for thee on the cross; that thou mightest also bear thy cross and desire to die on the cross with Him.

For if thou be dead with Him, thou shalt also live with Him. And if thou be His companion in punishment, thou shalt be partaker with Him also in glory.

Behold! In the cross all doth consist, and all lieth in our dying thereon; for there is no other way unto life, and unto true inward peace, but the way of the holy cross....Go where thou wilt, seek whatsoever thou wilt, thou shalt not find a higher way above, nor a safer way below, than the way of the holy cross.

THOMAS Á KEMPIS

The Imitation of Christ

FREE

FRANCINE RIVERS

I am free! Sin no longer has power over me! Jesus no longer hangs upon the cross for He is alive and I am alive in Him. I am His because of the gift of faith. He is my bread and water. He is the air I breathe. Let me be soft clay in Your mighty hands, Lord. Knead me and shape me into the vessel You intend me to be. For I experience the wonder of Your presence through the cross. Oh, the joy, the joy of my salvation through Jesus Christ, the Lord.

No pain, no palm; no thorns, no throne; no gall, no glory; no cross, no crown.

WILLIAM PENN

The Vigilance

Because of the CROSS

BONNIE KEEN

Although our churches are often decorated with beautiful, ornate crosses, the essence of what the cross means is found in its ugliness. There He hung, drenched in sweat, the joints of His body agonizingly pulling apart, gasping for breath and, finally, giving up His life for mine. It was God's unimaginable love that kept Jesus nailed to that rough-hewn, splintered wood for the sake of this fallen world. He suffered as one of us, with bones and sinews and muscles that strained and ached. He felt the loneliness of abandonment, the hurt of betrayal. And yet His love reached out to us.

What kind of love is this? It is a love beyond all reason, beyond anything we could ever deserve. His love reached out to us. It reaches out to us still.

The message that cries out from the cross is the message of hope. Death has been conquered. I am forgiven and free. I can face tomorrow. Because of His great love on that blood-soaked, sin-splattered wood, I know I am loved beyond measure, beyond failure, beyond disease, beyond all my unanswerable questions.

My only proper response can be trust. In my darkest moments, in my deepest pain, there lives in me and with me the One who died for me, One whose hand I can hold onto even when life seems to be tumbling down around me like a house of cards.

Because of the cross, I live and have hope.

He took my cross for His own;

I must take His Cross as my own;

I must be crucified   with Him.

It is as

I abide daily,   deeply in

Jesus the   Crucified

One, that I   shall taste

the sweetness of   His love, the

power of His life,

the completeness of His salvation.

ANDREW MURRAY

The Shadow